3/12/14

W9-CRV-692

CHILDREN IN HISTORY
Greeks

Kate Jackson Bedford

SEA-TO-SEA
Mankato Collingwood London

This edition first published in 2011 by
Sea-to-Sea Publications
Distributed by Black Rabbit Books
P.O. Box 3263, Mankato, Minnesota 56002

Copyright © Sea-to-Sea Publications 2011

Printed in China, Dongguan

All rights reserved.

Library of Congress Cataloging-in-Publication Data

Bedford, Kate.
  Greeks / Kate Jackson Bedford.
     p. cm. -- (Children in history)
  Includes index.
  ISBN 978-1-59771-270-5 (library binding)
 1. Children--Greece--Social life and customs--Juvenile literature.
[1. Greece--Social life and customs--To 146 B.C.--Juvenile
literature.] I. Title.
  DF77.B45 2011
  938--dc22

                                    2009044872

9 8 7 6 5 4 3 2

Published by arrangement with the Watts Publishing
Group Ltd, London.

Series editor: Jeremy Smith
Art director: Jonathan Hair
Design: Jane Hawkins
Cover design: Jane Hawkins
Picture research: Diana Morris

Picture credits: Ace Stock/Alamy: 21b. Alinari/Topfoto: 13.
Archeological Museum Bari/Gianni dagli Orti/Art Archive: 9,
30c. Archeological Museum Istanbul/Gianni dali Orti/Art
Archive: 16cr. Archeological Museum Izmir/dali Orti/Art
Archive: 7b, 30t. Archeological Museum Salonika/Gianni dagli
Orti/Art Archive: 18tl, 30b.Ashmolean Museum University of
Oxford/Bridgeman Art Library: 19t, 21t. Bettmann/Corbis: 25.
Bridgeman Art Library/Getty Images: 1,11, 12cr, 22b. Trustees of
the British Museum London: front cover tl, 7t, 23. British
Museum, London/Bridgeman Art Library: 4. British
Museum/HIP/Topfoto: front cover tr. DK Images: 2, 24bl.
Werner Forman Archive: front cover tc, b, 24cr. Fitzwilliam
Museum University of Cambridge/Bridgeman Art Library: 5b,
20, 28. Galleria degli Uffizi Florence/Bridgeman Art Library: 5t.
The Gallery Collection/Corbis: 12bl, 30ca. Lebrecht Music & Arts
PL/Alamy: 17. Fions Leewenberg/Corbis: 10cr. Araldo de
Luca/Corbis: 6bl. Musée du Louvre Paris/Erich Lessing/AKG
Images: 22t. Musée Municipal Antoine Vivenel
Compiegne/Lauros/Giraudon/Bridgeman Art Library: 26bl.
National Archeological Museum Athens/Gianni dagli Orti/Art
Archive: 10bl, 26cr. North Wind Picture/AKG Images: 27.
Gianni dagli Orti/Corbis: 3, 6r. Picturepoint/ Topfoto: 16bl, 29.
Ann Ronan PL/HIP/Topfoto: 18br. R Sheridan/AAA collection:
15. Vianni Archive/Corbis: 8t, 14c.

Every attempt has been made to clear copyright. Should there be
any inadvertent omission please apply to the publisher for
rectification.

March 2010
RD/6000006414/002

Note to parents and teachers: Every effort has been made
by the publishers to ensure that the web sites at the back
of the book are suitable for children, that they are of the
highest educational value, and that they contain no
inappropriate material. However, because of the nature of
the Internet, it is impossible to guarantee that the contents
of these sites will not be altered. We strongly advise that
Internet access is supervised by a responsible adult.

Contents

The Ancient Greeks

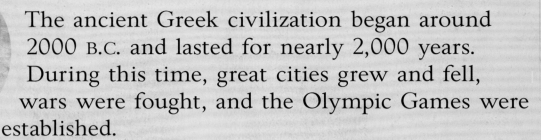

The ancient Greek civilization began around 2000 B.C. and lasted for nearly 2,000 years. During this time, great cities grew and fell, wars were fought, and the Olympic Games were established.

Greek Lands

The ancient Greeks lived in the country of Greece. This was made up of a mainland and many islands scattered throughout the Adriatic, Ionian, and Aegean seas. The land was mountainous and rocky, with only a small amount of flat land in narrow strips along the coast.

▶ This map shows where the ancient Greeks lived. The green areas were controlled by Athens and the red areas were allied states.

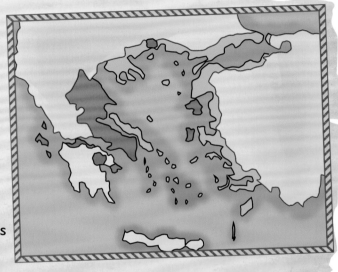

City-States

Ancient Greece was not a single country. It was made up of several hundred city-states. These were small self-governing cities that controlled the area surrounding them. Each city-state was independent and had its own rules, laws, army, and money. Quarrels between city-states over land or trade were common, and often led to wars.

◀ The decoration on this vase shows ancient Greek soldiers preparing for war.

The End of the Ancient Greeks

The era of the ancient Greeks came to an end as the Roman Empire expanded. The Greeks fought against the invading Romans but were eventually conquered. Greece finally came under Roman rule as part of the Roman Empire in 146 B.C. The Romans greatly admired many aspects of Greek life and copied such things as their alphabet and architecture.

▼ This sixteenth-century Renaissance painting shows the Greeks fighting the Romans using a "death ray" machine, invented by the scientist Archimedes (287–212 B.C.).

Children's Lives

Children's lives depended on how wealthy their family was, which city-state they lived in, and whether they were a boy or a girl. Girls were less valued than boys and in most city-states were fed less than their brothers. Only the boys of wealthy families were educated and poor children went to work from an early age.

▶ We can see what ancient Greek children looked like from the statues the Greeks left behind.

Family Life

Greek children grew up in a household with lots of people. They lived with their parents, brothers, sisters, grandparents, unmarried aunts, and slaves (see page 23). The children's father was in charge of everyone living in the home.

Surviving Childhood

In ancient Greece, many babies died at birth or within the first few days of life. Children who did survive often died later on from deadly diseases such as tuberculosis, malaria, and dysentery. Only half of the children who survived birth reached the age of 18.

▲ In this vase painting, a father decides whether to accept his new baby into the family.

Allowed to Live?

Babies who survived birth were inspected by their fathers to check if they were healthy enough to be accepted into the family. Children who were weak, sickly, or deformed were abandoned on a hillside. Once a baby was accepted into the family, it was given a name and treated kindly.

▲ This ancient Greek carving shows a child being examined by a doctor.

Potty Time

We know that young Greek children used large clay potties from examples dug up in archeological excavations and from pictures painted on vases. As well as being used for toilet training, the potty-chair was used as a highchair and a safe place to keep the baby from harm (or from making mischief) in the house.

▶ This vase painting shows a child sitting in a potty-chair, which also acts as a high chair.

Looking After the Children

Greek children from wealthy families were looked after by their mother or a stepmother, as well as grandmothers, aunts, and female slaves. They spent most of their time with their mother in the women's part of the home (see page 8). When boys reached the age of seven, they went out to school each day, but their sisters remained at home.

◀ Children spent most of their time with the women of the family.

At Home

The homes Greek children lived in depended on how rich their family was and if they lived in the town or the countryside. Most Greek homes were built of sun-dried mud bricks, painted white on the outside.

Home Design

Most Greek children lived in single-story homes with thick walls, a clay-tiled roof, and small, shuttered windows set high up in the walls. Each house had an open courtyard in the center with rooms arranged around it. The homes of rich families followed the same design but were larger, with more rooms.

▲ A sixth century B.C. model of the side of a Greek courtyard, showing a woman and child by the entrance.

▼ The white walls of Greek houses reflected the heat of the sun, helping to keep them cool.

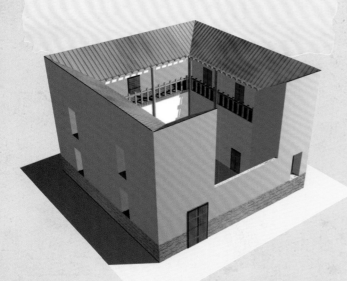

Separate Areas

Children were normally kept out of the dining room, which was the grandest room in a house. This was mainly used by their father to entertain guests. Women had their own separate area of the home called the gynaeceum, where they had their weaving looms, couches, and beds. Young children spent most of their time in the women's area or the courtyard.

In the Courtyard

Girls, women, and young children spent a lot of time in the courtyard. It was a light and airy place to work in warm weather. They did messy tasks, such as the laundry, in the courtyard and often cooked meals there using portable hearths. The courtyard was a safe place for young children to play while their mother worked nearby.

◀ This vase painting shows a boy slave collecting water. Some courtyards had a water well.

Villa of Good Fortune

Archeologists have discovered the remains of some ancient Greek homes, including the Villa of Good Fortune at Olynthos. The wealthy children who once lived here would have walked over beautiful mosaic floors. We can see how the rooms were arranged around the courtyard.

▶ This plan shows the ground floor of the Villa of Good Fortune.

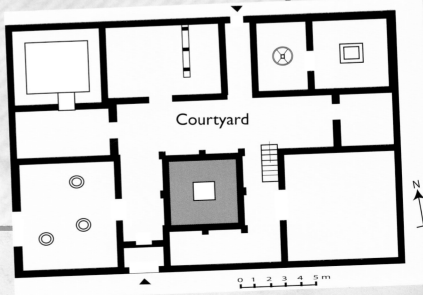

Courtyard

N

0 1 2 3 4 5 m

9

A Girl's Life

Girls living in ancient Greece were treated differently to boys. They could be seen as a burden to their family because parents had to give a gift of money or land, called a dowry, to the family of their husband-to-be when they married.

How to Behave

Girls were brought up to be obedient and to do as they were told. This would help them when they were adults and their lives were under the control of their husband. It was considered respectable for Greek women and girls to stay inside the house, so girls had to keep close to home.

▶ This statue shows an ancient Greek girl. Girls were taught to be obedient to their husbands.

◀ These statues show girls doing the household jobs of cooking and washing. ▶

Running a Home

All Greek girls learned how to run a home. Their mothers taught them how to spin, weave, clean, and cook. Even rich girls had to learn these skills so they could supervise their slaves. Girls also learned how to dance and sing secret songs to take part in religious festivals.

10

End of Childhood

A girl's childhood ended at around the age of 13, when her body had grown and changed so that she could have babies of her own. To celebrate this, girls took their toys to the Temple of Artemis and dedicated them to the goddess, who was believed to protect women in childbirth. After this, a girl would marry a man chosen by her father.

Serving a Goddess

Some young Athenian girls between the ages of seven and ten spent a year living at the Temple of Artemis in Brauron, near Athens. They worked as attendants and did tasks such as weaving and sacred dancing. The girls also took part in a ritual involving dancing or running around the altar at a service called "playing the bear." This ritual symbolized the "taming of a woman" before she took her wedding vows.

▲ Athenian girls taking part in the "playing the bear" service would have looked similar to this statue.

Greek Boys

Ancient Greek boys lived a much more active life than girls. They were more valued in their family because they carried on the family name, could inherit property, and would grow up to become soldiers.

In the Army

War was a normal part of ancient Greek life. Boys trained to be physically fit and able to fight. They were expected to join the army when they grew up. During a war, boys helped defend their city by carrying ammunition to the front line.

▶ This carving shows boys playing sports to help them grow into soldiers.

Olympic Games

Boys between the ages of 12 and 17 were allowed to take part in the Olympic Games, which were held every four years. They competed in competitions including running, wrestling, and boxing. To make the contests fairer, boys competed in classes that were divided according to the boys' ages, strength, and physical size.

◀ This vase is decorated with young men taking part in a race.

Becoming a Man

On the island of Crete, boys took part in a ritual to leave behind their childhood. First, they spent time acting as a servant for rich men and then they were taught how to fight. At the end of this time, they took part in the Undressing Festival, where they cast off the shabby clothes worn during their training and put on new adult clothes.

▶ This frieze shows a boy about to receive his new clothes and become a man in the Undressing Festival.

GREEK LEGACY

Modern Olympics

The first Olympic Games were held in 776 B.C. and every four years afterward until A.D. 394, when they were abolished by the Romans. In 1896, a Frenchman, Pierre de Coubertin, decided to revive the games. The first modern Olympic Games were held in Athens in 1896. They have been held all around the world every four years since then, except during World Wars I and II.

The Spartan Way

The powerful Greek city-state of Sparta was a superpower whose main aim was to be ready for war. Boys and girls growing up there were trained from an early age to be soldiers, or the mothers of soldiers.

▲ Spartan mothers washed their babies in wine. They believed it would make them stronger.

Being Born a Spartan

Every baby born in Sparta was owned by the state and not its parents. Sparta only wanted healthy babies, so state officials decided if a newborn baby was strong enough to be kept. Weak babies were left to die of starvation or cold on a mountainside.

Tough Training

At the age of seven, all boys left home and went to live in military barracks where life was harsh. Boys went barefoot, only had a cloak to wear, and were kept so hungry that most stole food. They were taught a little reading and writing, but mainly did sports and trained to be soldiers.

GREEK LEGACY

Don't Get Caught

Spartan boys who were discovered stealing food were badly beaten, not because they were stealing but because they were caught. A story from 75 B.C. tells us about a Spartan boy who stole a fox to eat and hid it under his cloak when he met some soldiers. While they questioned him, the fox chewed into his stomach, but the boy didn't show any sign of pain because it would have given him away. He later died from his wounds.

Strong Girls

Spartan girls were trained to have a healthy body so they would have strong babies when they grew up. They did sports such as running, wrestling, dancing, and gymnastics, as well as learning household skills from their mothers. Spartan girls had much more freedom than girls in other parts of Greece.

▶ This bronze statue shows a strong and healthy Spartan girl.

Mealtimes

Greek children ate a healthy diet with plenty of fresh fruit and vegetables. Many families ate food they had grown themselves or that came from the animals they kept. Children helped to grow, harvest, and prepare food.

On the Menu

Children ate lots of bread made from wheat or barley, as well as dried beans, peas, and lentils, cheese, eggs, and honey, and fruit and vegetables including apples, pears, pomegranates, cherries, onions, carrots, and spinach. Meals often included seafood such as octopus, squid, fish, or shellfish.

▲ The ancient Greeks ate with their hands and used bread to soak up soups.

▲ This vase is decorated with an octopus, a popular Greek seafood.

Healthy Food

For breakfast children usually ate bread dipped in olive oil, and fruit. Lunch was more bread with olives, figs, and goat cheese. The main meal of the day was eaten at sunset when they had barley porridge or more bread with beans and vegetables, fish, fruit, and honey cakes. Children drank wine mixed with water.

Not Much Meat

Eating meat at festivals was a special treat for children. The Greeks believed it was wrong to kill and eat a domestic animal, such as a goat or a sheep, without sacrificing it to the gods first. At festivals, they sacrificed animals and afterward the meat was cooked for everyone to eat.

▼ The bull in this vase painting is about to be sacrificed to the gods.

GREEK LEGACY

Still Eaten Today

The foods eaten by the ancient Greeks are still eaten in Greece today and they are also enjoyed by people all around the world. Feta cheese, olives, figs, and even foods such as octopus and squid can be bought in many supermarkets. Many people cook using olive oil and enjoy drinking wine with their meals, just like the Greeks.

Going to School

Most Greek children didn't go to school. Only boys from wealthy families went to school and lessons had to be paid for. Girls stayed at home and were taught how to look after the house and family by their mothers and grandmothers.

▲ Boys sat on benches facing the teacher.

At School

Boys usually started school when they were seven years old. They were taught in classes of up to 12 pupils by three different types of teacher. One teacher taught arithmetic, reading, writing, and poetry, another helped boys learn to play musical instruments and sing, and a third taught sports, such as wrestling, gymnastics, and athletics.

School Slave

Some boys were taken to school by a trusted slave called a paidogogos. This slave sat behind the boy in his lessons and made sure that he behaved well and concentrated on his work. Any misbehavior or lack of studying would be reported back to the boy's parents.

▼ This vase painting shows boys being taught music and writing. The paidogogos (sitting on the right) watches the lessons.

Writing Materials

Boys wrote on wooden tablets covered with beeswax. They used a stylus made from wood or bone to carve letters into the wax. After their work was finished, they smoothed over the wax with the wide end of the stylus and the tablet could be used again. Boys also wrote on papyrus scrolls using reed pens dipped in ink.

▶ These pieces of papyrus were bound together to make a book.

GREEK LEGACY

Words and Letters

The alphabet we use today is adapted from the one used by the ancient Greeks. The Romans adapted the Greek alphabet to write their language Latin, and it is this alphabet that we use today. The word alphabet comes from the first two letters of the Greek alphabet, "alpha" and "beta." Many other words we use every day come from Greek words, for example, micro comes from "mircros" meaning small.

▶ The Greek alphabet had 24 letters.

A	B	Γ	Δ	E	Z
ALPHA	BETA	GAMMA	DELTA	EPSILON	ZETA
H	Θ	I	K	Λ	M
ETA	THETA	IOTA	KAPPA	LAMBDA	MU
N	Ξ	O	Π	P	Σ
NU	XI	OMICRON	PI	RHO	SIGMA
T	Y	Φ	X	Ψ	Ω
TAU	UPSILON	PHI	CHI	PSI	OMEGA

What to Wear

Greek children dressed in similar clothes to their parents. Their clothes were comfortable, loose, and flowing—perfect for the hot weather in Greece. Children's clothes were made at home by their mothers, slaves, and sisters.

Greek Style

Boys and girls wore a tunic called a chiton. It was made from a rectangle of cloth that was folded, sewn up at the sides, pinned into place on the shoulders, and gathered around the waist with a soft belt. Girls wore white, ankle-length chitons. Boys' chitons were knee length. In colder weather, children also wore a cloak or a shawl.

▶ The girl in this statue is wearing a chiton, which was made from linen or light wool.

SIFTING THE EVIDENCE

New Clothes for a Goddess

The carved frieze around the Parthenon in Athens, a temple dedicated to the goddess Athene, shows girls presenting the goddess with a new chiton. The girls had also woven the cloth for the chiton because they were seen to be innocent and pure, making them the best people for the job.

From Top to Toe

In some parts of Greece, boys grew their hair long and braided it to keep it out of the way. In other places they had short hair. Girls wore their hair long and kept it in braids or ponytails, and decorated it with ribbons. Most Greek children went barefoot, but some wore leather shoes or sandals.

◀ Statues show us how children wore their hair in ancient Greece.

No Clothes

At school, boys didn't change into different clothes for their physical education classes—they did them naked. Taking part in running, boxing, and wrestling with no clothes on was considered normal in ancient Greece. After exercise, boys rubbed olive oil onto their skin to keep it supple and remove the dirt.

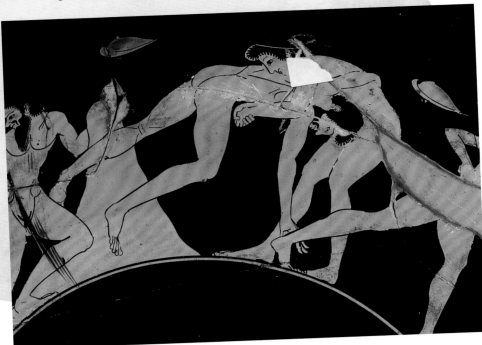

▶ The decoration on this Greek vase shows men wrestling naked.

21

At Work

Most children had to work in ancient Greece. In poor families, children had to start helping to run the family home, farm, or business from an early age. Some of the poorest children were slaves.

Family Business

Children helped their parents with jobs at the family business or farm. The sons of craftsmen, such as potters, blacksmiths, or shoemakers, became apprentices and learned to do the same job as their father. Farmer's children helped out by picking stones out of fields, scaring birds off the crops, and bringing in the harvest.

▲ This vase painting shows how children climbed up trees to harvest the fruit.

▼ This statue shows girls making bread.

Getting the Work Done

Boys and girls did different jobs in the family. Girls ground wheat into flour for making bread. They also helped their mothers bake, milk the goats, make cheese, press olives for oil, and gather nuts and berries. Boys did more outside jobs such as running errands, collecting fuel, and herding goats.

Being a Slave

Many Greek families owned slaves. Child slaves may have been born into slavery because their parents were slaves, or they may have been abandoned as babies, and then rescued and brought up as a slave. Some slave children were kidnapped by slave traders or captured in wartime.

▼ This painting shows a slave girl dancing to entertain a young man at a symposium.

Slave Entertainers

Scenes painted on Greek vases show us that slave girls worked at men's banquets or drinking parties, called symposia. Respectable women were not allowed to go to symposia. Slave girls, known as hetairai, were used to entertain the men with dancing, music, and acrobatic displays. Many hetairai were prisoners captured during wars.

Toys and Games

Ancient Greek children played with toys made from wood, clay, or even bone. Many of their toys were made at home by members of the family. Wealthy families bought toys from craftsmen.

Toys

Young children played with rattles, dolls, dolls' houses, model animals, and hobby horses. Older children enjoyed games with tops, kites, hoops, yo-yos, and small carts. They used nuts to play games similar to marbles and a blown-up pig's bladder covered in leather to play ball games.

◀ Toys, such as this horse and rider, were made from clay.

▲ This statue shows girls enjoying a game of knucklebones.

Knucklebones

Greek children played with knucklebones, which were cleaned ankle-joint bones from small animals, such as goats or sheep. They used knucklebones to play several different games. One game involved throwing a knucklebone into the air, and picking up another from the ground before catching the thrown one. This was repeated with the player having to quickly pick up two knucklebones, then three, and so on.

Story Time

Children still read stories today that were written by Aesop, a Greek slave, about 2,500 years ago. He wrote more than 650 short stories, called fables, which remind people how to behave well. For example, Aesop wrote the story of the tortoise and the hare, which shows that it is better to work slowly and carefully, than quickly and carelessly.

Pets

Many Greek children kept animals as pets. Birds, dogs, and rabbits were the most popular. Some children kept tortoises, mice, insects such as grasshoppers, and even monkeys. Children had toy carts with a small harness that they could attach to dogs and be pulled around by them.

◀ This beautiful Greek tombstone shows a Greek girl playing with pet birds.

Festivals and Ceremonies

In ancient Greece, people held festivals and religious ceremonies to worship their gods and goddesses. Children played an important role in festivals by helping to perform rituals.

Girls' Role

Girls with both parents still living were considered to be the best people to help with religious ceremonies. Their role was to grind grain to make special cakes for the gods, to wash the statue of the god, or carry special olive branches in processions.

▶ The girls in this wall painting are carrying olive branches in a procession.

Wine Festival

When boys reached the age of three, they took part in a spring festival called Anthesteria, which was held in honor of Dionysus, the wine god. It marked the end of a boy's babyhood and was the first stage toward becoming a man. Boys were taken to a temple where they had their first sips of wine.

◀ Small wine cups like this were given to boys to celebrate taking part in the festival.

Safely Swinging

Every spring in Athens, young girls took part in a swinging ritual called the Aiora. It commemorated the death of a girl named Erigone, who had taken her own life after finding her father dead. Swings were tied to trees and the idea was that, unlike Erigone, the girls would play safely and enjoy swinging from the branches of trees.

▶ A Victorian painting shows the Aiora swinging ritual.

The Parthenon

The Parthenon still stands on a hill above modern Athens. Children of ancient Greece took part in processions and rituals to the goddess Athene (see page 20) at this temple. The Parthenon is made of white marble and has columns and statues. A large frieze decorates the sides of the temple and shows the procession during a festival in honor of Athene.

Activities

Try some games or other activities relating to the ancient Greeks.

Play Ephedrismos

Ephedrismos is an ancient Greek piggyback game. All you need to play is a tall stone and two players. This game should only be played with adult supervision.

- Balance a tall stone upright on the ground.

- Each player takes turns to throw a ball or a pebble at the stone to try to knock it over.

- The person who knocks the stone over first becomes the piggyback rider and the other player is the carrier.

- The carrier can only hold onto one of the rider's legs. The rider is allowed to cling onto the carrier.

- While the carrier is giving a piggyback ride, he has to try to touch the stone with one hand and still keep his balance so the rider does not fall off.

- To make it even harder, the rider can cover the carrier's eyes with his or her hands.

Ancient Greek Style

Make a simple Greek tunic. You will need an old sheet, safety pins, and a belt.

- Fold the sheet so it is long enough to reach from shoulder to knees for a boy, or shoulder to ankles for a girl.

- Wrap the sheet around your body loosely and use safety pins to hold it together over each shoulder.

- Close the open side with more pins.

- Tie a belt around your waist.

- Go barefoot or wear leather sandals.

Read some Ancient Greek Stories

If you like exciting adventure stories, read some Greek myths or legends. Find out about Hercules and his 12 difficult labors, Perseus tackling the monstrous snake-headed Medusa, who turned people to stone with one glance, and the many adventures of Odysseus on his way home from the Trojan War. Try some of Aesop's fables too—there are plenty to choose from.

Try some Greek Food

Why not try some Greek foods you've never eaten before? Look for olives, feta cheese, figs, and octopus in your local grocery store. Use them to prepare some ancient Greek-style meals.

Cook Like an Ancient Greek

Try this recipe for an ancient Greek-style fruit salad.

Ingredients:

- 1 melon
- 2 peaches
- 2 pears
- 1 bunch of seedless grapes
- $\frac{1}{4}$ cup chopped almonds (optional)
- 5 tablespoons of honey
- 2 glasses of grape or apple juice

Method:

- Cut the melon in half and carefully remove and discard the seeds. Then cut out the melon flesh and slice it into small pieces. Place it in a bowl.

- Wash the rest of the fruit and cut it into pieces. Add to the bowl along with the almonds.

- Put the honey and the apple or grape juice in a pan. Ask an adult to warm this through over low heat until the honey has dissolved.

- Pour this syrup over the fruit. Cover and place in the refrigerator to chill for one hour before serving.

Timeline

(ca. before a date means "circa," which means "around that time.")

ca. 2000 B.C. Minoan civilization flourishes on the island of Crete.

ca. 1600 B.C. Mycenaeans are a powerful group on the Greek mainland.

ca. 1450 B.C. Mycenaeans invade and conquer Crete.

ca. 1250 B.C. The Trojan War—the Greeks use a huge wooden horse to trick the Trojans.

ca. 1100 B.C. The Mycenaean civilization declines.

ca. 800 B.C. Greek culture starts to flourish again.

700s B.C. Greece is divided into independent city-states.

776 B.C. First Olympic Games are held at Olympia.

ca. 700 B.C. The poet Homer composes *The Iliad* and *The Odyssey*.

ca. 500 B.C. Democracy begins in Athens.

490-449 B.C. Persian wars. The Greeks defeat the Persians at the Battle of Marathon.

472-410 B.C. Greek theater thrives in Athens.

432 B.C. The Parthenon is finished.

431-404 B.C. Peloponnesian War between Athens and Sparta. Sparta wins.

371 B.C. Thebes defeats Sparta and becomes the leading Greek power.

362 B.C. Sparta and Athens join together to defeat Thebes.

338 B.C. King Philip of Macedonia takes control of Greece.

336 B.C. Alexander the Great becomes king of Macedonia.

330 B.C. Aristole invents the camera obscura.

215 B.C. Archimedes invents the catapult, which is used to stop the Romans from invading.

147-146 B.C. The Achaean War—the Romans conquer Greece.

146 B.C. Greece becomes part of the Roman Empire.

A.D. 394 Romans stop the Olympic Games.

Glossary and Further information

ammunition arrows or stones fired from a weapon.

apprentice young person who is taught a craft, such as blacksmithing, and in return works for his instructor for a number of years.

architecture the style and design of buildings.

Artemis goddess of hunting, childbirth, the young, and wild animals.

Athene goddess of wisdom, skills, and war.

civilization an organized society of people. Civilizations have their own laws, religions, and ways of writing.

climate weather conditions of an area.

conquer overpower a country in war and then take charge of it.

domesticated tame animals that live with or are kept by people.

dowry money or property given by a woman's family to the family of the husband she is marrying.

frieze horizontal strip of pattern or sculpture around a room or building.

malaria disease caused by a bite from an infected mosquito.

mosaic pattern made from small pieces of different colored stones or tiles.

papyrus paper made from an Egyptian sedge plant.

ritual a religious ceremony.

sacrifice to kill an animal as a gift to the gods.

squid a sea animal with tentacles, also called a cuttlefish.

Finding Out More about Life in Ancient Greece

There are museums and web sites you can visit to find out more about ancient Greek children.

www.getty.edu/art/exhibitions/coming_of_age/home.html
Learn how to play knucklebones, listen to children speaking about life in ancient Greece, and hear music played on Greek instruments.

http://greece.mrdonn.org/
Find out everything you could possibly want to know about the ancient Greeks.

http://historylink102.com/greece3/children.htm
This site has lots of information on daily life in ancient Greece, including the lives of children. Visit the site to find out about home life, shopping, fashion, and much more.

www.ancientgreece.co.uk/
This site has lots of information on life in ancient Greece. Visit the site to explore the inside of a Greek house, try building your own Greek temple, or take the challenge game to live the harsh life of a Spartan boy.

Index